NINE SEPHARDIC SONGS

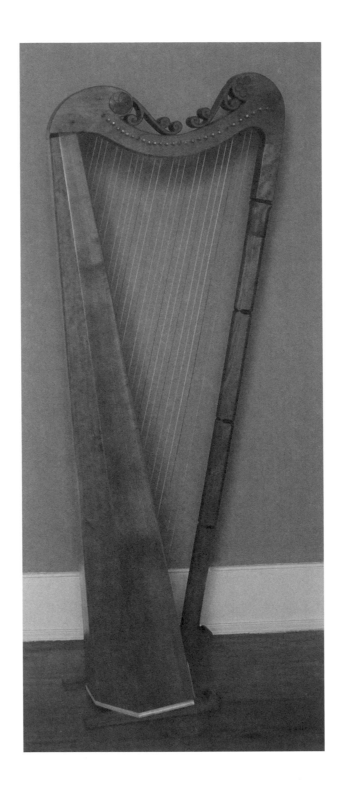

An Iberian single-strung stave-back diatonic harp—*arpa de una orden*—copied from a mid-seventeenth century Colombian original, made by Lynne Lewandowski, Bellows Falls, Vermont. The range is from second octave C to sixth octave C. It stands 59 inches tall, 21 inches wide, with a sounding board 11-1/2 inches wide at the bottom. There is no provision for chromatic changes during the course of the music, but the use of scordatura tuning is an effective solution to the problem. The harpist stands while playing. The gut strings are quite thin, so they are played near the top to make them feel firmer under the fingers.

NINE SEPHARDIC SONGS

arranged for

voice and harp

by

Samuel Milligan

Ars Musicæ Hispaniæ

a division of

WingsPress

San Antonio, Texas

Cover illustration: Jewish scholars in procession, 1417.
Rosgartenmuseum, Konstanz, Germany.

First Edition

Spiral bound Edition ISBN: 978-1-60940-453-6

Ebook editions:
ePub ISBN: 978-1-60940-454-3
MobiPocket/Kindle ISBN: 978-1-60940-455-0
Library PDF ISBN: 978-1-60940-456-7

Wings Press
627 E. Guenther
San Antonio, Texas 78210
Phone/fax: (210) 271-7805
On-line catalogue and ordering:www.wingspress.com
All Wings Press titles are distributed to the trade by
Independent Publishers Group
www.ipgbook.com

With thanks to Gordon Johnston for invaluable graphic assistance.

for
Diane Golkin

Contents

INTRODUCTION:
THE MUSIC OF THE SEPHARDIM

Jews probably first arrived in Spain in Roman times. The Iberian peninsula is called *Sepharad* in Hebrew, so the Spanish Jews have come to be called the Sephardim or, in Spanish, Sefardi.

They probably did not fare well when Visogothic Spain became Christian, but conditions improved when the Muslims conquered the country, resulting in a golden age of Sephardic learning, art and literature. For example, they played an important part in translating several works from antiquity—such as Aristotle—from Arabic into Latin, the intellectual language of the Christians of Western Europe, thus preventing their loss. The Sephardim were important as doctors, astronomers and poets, such as the doctor/philosopher Maimonides [1135 – 1204], and the poets Salomon Ibn Gabirol [c.1020 – c.1057] and Judah Halevi [c.1075 – c.1141].

But after the long and bitter *Reconquista,* the Christians were again in power in Spain, and in no mood to tolerate unbelievers of any stripe, and so in 1492 the "Catholic Monarchs," Fernando and Isabel issued an Edict of Expulsion—the so-called Alhambra Decree—which ruled that all Muslims and Jews who would not convert had 30 days in which to leave the country or be executed. They could take nothing with them other than what they were wearing.

BAD TIMES

The immediate effect of this tragic and ill-advised action was a serious economic recession. More importantly, it was a blow to the intellectual and artistic life of the country, a fact that was known at least to the Ottoman sultan, Bayezid II, who ridiculed the Catholic Monarchs for expelling so useful a population. "You venture to call Fernando a wise ruler," he said to his courtiers—"he who impoverished his own country and enriched mine." Beyezid instructed his subjects to welcome the exiles, settling them in various places in the Ottoman Empire. Unfortunately, in other lands, many Sephardim were received with hostility. Some were captured and sold into slavery by pirates—mainly from Genoa—and still others, sad to relate, finding no place to go, starved to death.

But a great many resettled in the Ottoman Empire, which at the time included Egypt and the Balkans. Notable settlements, at least musically, were Smyrna (now Izmir), Saloniki, Alexandria and the Island of Rhodos. Other Sefardi went to North Africa, Germany, England, the Low Countries, Southern France and Italy. (The Italian word *ghetto* comes from the name of a specific neighborhood in Rome where the Sephardim settled).

A NEW WORLD

At the time of the expulsion, any Jew who would accept Catholic Christianity would be allowed to stay in Spain. Faced with the bleak conditions forced on exiles, about half accepted baptism in order to stay. Called *conversos*, they had a rather rough time of it, since the Inquisition suspected them of still practicing Judaism in secret, which, of course, many did. Ordinarily, the *conversos* were not allowed to leave Spain, though some were allowed to settle in what is now south Texas in order to create a buffer population between northern New Spain and hostile Apache and Comanche Indians.

Others, astonishingly enough, found homes in the mountains of northern New Mexico and southern Colorado, doubtless to get as far away as possible from the Inquisition which had established an ugly presence in Mexico. There is a musical connection here, since similarities have been found between the Sephardic cantorial style and the *alabados* of the *penitente* brotherhoods of New Mexico and Colorado.

Prompted in part by verification of their ancestry by DNA research, some descendants of these same New Mexican *conversos* have returned to Judaism. Others remain committed Roman Catholics while continuing Jewish practices, such as avoiding pork, lighting sabbath candles and the like, by this time regarding them as family traditions rather than religious practices.

Certain Spanish family names in the southwest reveal a possible Sephardic origin, such as Méndez, Moreno, Vargas, Mejia, Muñoz, Salinas and Sanchez.

APOLOGY AND REHABILITATION

In 1992, five hundred years after the Edict of Expulsion, the Spanish king, Juan Carlos, speaking at a synagogue in Toledo, made an apology for the expulsion. An effort was begun in 2012 to make possible the return of *converso* descendants to Spanish citizenship. This became official in 2014. Conversos who can demonstrate their qualifications can apply for dual citizenship, maintaining that of their home country as well as that of Spain. In Spain there is a rising feeling of pride in the Sephardic contribution to Spanish history and culture.

LADINO = JUDEZMO = ESPANYOL

Among the things the Sephardim took with them in their diaspora was their language. This is most commonly called Ladino, though that name originally belonged to vernacular translations of Hebrew religious texts, utilizing the Hebrew alphabet. The popular language should more properly be called Judezmo, but the term Ladino has come to prevail. It is based very largely on 15th Century Castilian with a sprinkling of Hebrew, Arabic, Greek, and Turkish words, depending on where the diaspora landed them.

Ladino, like Spanish, is a strikingly beautiful language—very musical—and so contributes to the beauty of Sephardic song. Some of this music may date its origins back to the time of the expulsion, but it is very difficult to decide just which, if any, actually do so. However, a study of variants can help in estimating age, as can the use of archaic language forms. Also, outside influences will indicate a later origin—earlier texts are less likely to include Greek, Turkish or Arabic words. Provenance is also important. If a song is found in several widely dispersed communities, such as say, Thessaloniki, Alexandria and Tunisia, it's possible that it could, at least in part, predate the 1492 diaspora.

Sephardic musical influence has been widespread. As noted above, the *alabados* of the *penitentes* of the American southwest show possible Sephardic characteristics. A more obvious connection can be made with *cante jondo,* the music of the gypsies of Andalusia. Note also the cantorial style of the *saetas* improvised by street singers during Holy Week processions in Seville. A particular characteristic is the frequent use of the harmonic minor scale with a raised 7th degree, which contributes a feeling of exotic sadness, particularly if the 4th degree is raised as well. But whatever scales are utilized, the result is a repertory of original and haunting beauty.

ALBERTO HEMSI

While Sephardic musical influences have been widespread, these are, in a sense, emanations from a core body of song, that, owing to the politics of the Near East, would most certainly have been lost, except for the labor and devotion of one remarkable man.

Alberto Hemsi was born on June 27th, 1898 from Italian Sephardic parents, in Kasaba (home of the famous melons), about 70 miles east of Smyrna. A notable early influence was his grandmother who shared her repertory of Sephardic songs. In 1913 he entered the conservatory in Milan, studying piano, theory and composition. As an Italian citizen, he was drafted into the army during the First World War where he received a wound in his right arm. After the army he decided to devote himself entirely to music.

After gaining his conservatory degree in 1919, Hemsi returned to his home in Turkey. Hearing the songs of his grandmother, he decided to begin collecting this music, realizing that otherwise it would be lost. He lived by teaching music in Smyrna until moving to Rhodos in 1923, where he taught and collected songs until 1927. In 1928 he was invited by a Sephardic congregation in Alexandria to serve as director of music, teaching also at the G. Verdi and Alexandria conservatories and collecting more folk material until 1957 when, because of political unrest, he moved to Paris where he became music director for two Sephardic congregations, Brith Shalom and Don Isaac Abravanel, at the same time teaching at the Séminaire Israélite de France. Shortly before his death in 1957 he was made a correspondent of the San Fernando Royal Academy of Arts in Madrid in honor of his work as a preserver and promoter of Sephardic music.

Alberto Hemsi's work is voluminous, consisting not only of songs for voice and piano, but works for choir, one and two pianos, violin or cello and piano, various ensembles and orchestra.

He is mostly heard today in his arrangements of Sephardic songs for voice and piano, in which folk material is left untouched, but encased in progressive harmonies that lift the whole into the category of art song, similar to the work done to folksong of various countries and cultures by such composers as Canteloube, Falla, Britten, Vaughan Williams, Niles, Barber and Orff. But Hemsi's major contribution to music is to have saved an immense treasury of Sephardic folk song from oblivion.

The words and melodies of this collection have been collated with Hemsi's collection.

ABOUT THE HARP

In arranging these songs, I chose the Spanish diatonic harp of the Renaissance-Baroque periods [*el arpa de una orden*] for the accompaniment. This instrument can make no chromatic changes once the scale has been set up in the beginning. Thus, harmonic needs may require the use of scordatura tuning. An example can be found in this collection, in the lament *Como la Rosa en la Guerta*, which requires a third octave G-sharp in the introductory measures, the other G's remaining natural. Scordatura tuning allows us to plan ahead.

Any harp can be used that has as large a range as the Spanish harp, C-II to C-VI. And while a Spanish type instrument would be ideal, these songs will find a happy home with a modern folk harp equipped with thin gauge strings, a type that can be readily found these days. Thin strings, installed on a harp with an unveneered sounding board, are capable of an infinite degree of precise articulation and beautifully shaded phrasing.

But most convenient will doubtless be the pedal harp. And barring all else, there's always the piano, I suppose.

WHY VOCAL MUSIC?

The music critic John Ardoin once pointed out to me that the history of western music is basically a history of vocal music. The voice is the ultimate musical instrument, and even in strictly instrumental pieces, we strive to use phrasing to imitate vocal breathing.

My own career as a musician came from being born into a family of singers who needed an accompanist. And an Irish father, devoted to Irish songs, meant a son equipped with a Clark Irish harp. The influence was a good one, because today my favorite music making is found in accompanying singers, whether on a one-on-one basis, or in an opera orchestra.

Consequently, I am always pleased to find interesting vocal literature of whatever provenance, and present it with harp accompaniment—to my ear, the most beautiful combination possible.

Samuel Milligan
Brooklyn, New York

NINE SEPHARDIC SONGS

Aquel Rey de Francia

Arranged by
Samuel Milligan

Anonymous

1.A - quel re de Fran - cia,— tres hi - jas
2.La u - na cor - ta - va,— la o - tra cu -

te - ni - a. La u - na cor - ta - va, y la o - tra cu - zi - a.
zi - a. La más chi - qui - ti - ca— bas - ti - dor ha - zi - a.

3.La mas chi - qui - ti - ca— bas - ti - dor ha - zi -

Aquel Rey de Francia

a, lav-ran-do, lav-ran - do el sue-ño le ve - ni - a.

mf
4.Lav-ran - do, lav-ran - do, __ sue-ño

la ve - ni - a. La ma-dre, con ra - via har-var le que-ri -

Aquel Rey de Francia

1. This king of France had three daughters.
   One cut, and another sewed.

2. The one cut, and another sewed.
   The youngest did embroidery.

3. The youngest did embroidery.
   Working, working, sleep overtook her.

4. Working, working, sleep overtook her.
   The mother, enraged, drove her on.

   The mother, enraged, drove her on.

Durme, Durme, Hermozo Hijico

Cradle Song

Arranged by
Samuel Milligan

Anonymous

Very tranquil ♩ = 60

Dur - me, dur - me her - mo - zo hi - ji - co, dur - me, dur - me

con sa - vor. Dur - me, dur - me, her - mo - zo hi - ji - co, dur - me, dur - me

con sa - vor. Ce - rra tus lu - zios o - ji - cos, dur - me, dur - me con sa -

Durme, Durme, Hermozo Hijico

vor.   Ce - rra tus lu-zios o - ji - cos, dur-me, dur-me con sa -

vor.   A la sco - la tu__ te i - ras, y la ley t'am be - za -

ras.   A la sco - la tu__ te i - ras, y la ley t'am be - za -

Durme, Durme, Hermozo Hijico

ras. Dur - me, dur - me her-mo - zo hi-ji - co, dur - me, dur - me

con sa - vor. Dur - me, dur - me, her-mo - zo hi-ji - co, dur - me, dur - me

con sa - vor. Ce - rra tus lu-zios o - ji - cos, dur-me, dur-me con sa -

Durme, Durme, Hermozo Hijico

vor. Ce - rra__ tus__ lu - zios o - ji - cos,

dur - me, dur - me con sa - vor.__

Sleep, sleep, beautiful little boy, sleep with pleasure. (2 times)

Close your shining eyes, sleep with pleasure. (2 times)

You will go to school, and you will study the law. (2 times)

Sleep, sleep, beautiful little boy, etc.

Cuando el Rey Nimrod al Compo Salia

Anonymous

Cuando el Rey Nimrod al Compo Salia

f Cuan-do el rey Nim-rod

al com-po sa-lí - a, mi - ra-va en el cie-lo y en la es-tre - lle - ri - a. Vi-do u-na luz san-

Cuando el Rey Nimrod al Compo Salia

ta en la ju - de - ri - a. Que ha - vi - a de na - cer.___ Av - ra - ham a -

vi - nu. Av - ram a - vi - nu, pa - dre que - ri - do, pa - dre ben -

Cuando el Rey Nimrod al Compo Salia

Cuando el Rey Nimrod al Compo Salia

de - mos a - go - ra al se - ñor pa - ri - do, que le se - a be - si - man - tov es -

te___ na - ci - do, E - li - a - hu ha - na - vi mos se - a a - pa - re - ci - do, y

Cuando el Rey Nimrod al Compo Salia

da - re - mos lo - a - res ____ al ____ ver - da - de - ro. Av - ram a -

vi - nu, pa - dre que - ri - do, pa - dre ben - di - cho, luz de - Is - ra -

Cuando el Rey Nimrod al Compo Salia

el. _____ Av-ram a - vi - nu, pa-dre que-ri - do, pa-dre ben-

di - cho, luz de Is-ra - el.   3.Sa - lu - de-mos al com-pa-dre

Cuando el Rey Nimrod al Compo Salia

y tam-bien al mo - el, que por su zek-hut mos ven-ga el go - el, y

ri' - ha - ma a to-do Is-ra-el. Ci - er - to___ lo - a - re-mos

Cuando el Rey Nimrod al Compo Salia

al ___ ver-da - de - ro. Av-ram a - vi - nu, pa-dre que-ri - do, pa-dre ben-

di - cho, luz de Is-ra - el. _____ Av-ram a - vi - nu, pa-dre que-

Cuando el Rey Nimrod al Compo Salia

ri - do, pa-dre ben - di - cho, luz de Is-ra - el.

1. When King Nimrod went out into the countryside,
   He looked at the sky and the constellations.
   He saw a sacred light over the Jewish quarter,
   That there would be born Abraham, our father.

   Abraham, our father, father beloved,
   Blessed father, light of Israel.

2. Let us now greet the newborn father.
   May he be blessed, this newborn son.
   The prophet Elijah has to us appeared.
   And we shall praise the true one.

   Abraham, our father, etc.

3. Greeting to the godfather and to the mohel,*
   For because of his virtue the Messiah comes.
   And to redeem all of Israel,
   Certainly we give praise to the true one.

   Abraham, our father, etc.

Note: *This song celebrates the welcoming of the newborn boy into the Jewish community by the rite of circumcision. In the second verse the boy is greeted as the newborn father of the next generation. The third verse reminds us that this boy just mght be the hoped-for Messiah.*

* Mohel — one who performs the circumcision.

Puncha, Puncha, la Rosa Huele

Arranged by
Samuel Milligan

Anonymous

Puncha, Puncha, la Rosa Huele

Puncha, Puncha, la Rosa Huele

Si o-tra vez me que-res ver_____ Sa-le a-fue-ra, te_____hay-la - ré. E-cha los o-jos a la mar;_____

Puncha, Puncha, la Rosa Huele

A - llí me pue - des en - con - trar.

[1 min. 53 sec.]

1. Stings, stings, the perfumed rose
   Because love hurts a lot.
   You were not meant for me.
   Quickly get away from me.

2. Remember that hour
   When I kissed your lips?
   That hour has passed.
   Sorrow remains in my heart.

3. If you want to see me again,
   Come outside and I'll speak with you.
   Turn your eyes to the sea.
   There you will find me.

Adio, Querido

Arranged by
Samuel Milligan

Anonymous

Adío, Querido

ma - dre cuan-do te par - ió,   y te qui-tó el mun - do,   co -
búx - ca te o-tro a - mor,   a - har - va o-tras puer - tas.   A -

ra - són e-lla no te dió.   pa - ra/a - mar se-gun - do.   Co -
spe - ra o-tro ar - dor,   que pa - ra mi sos muer - ta.   A -

Adio, Querido

Adio, Querido

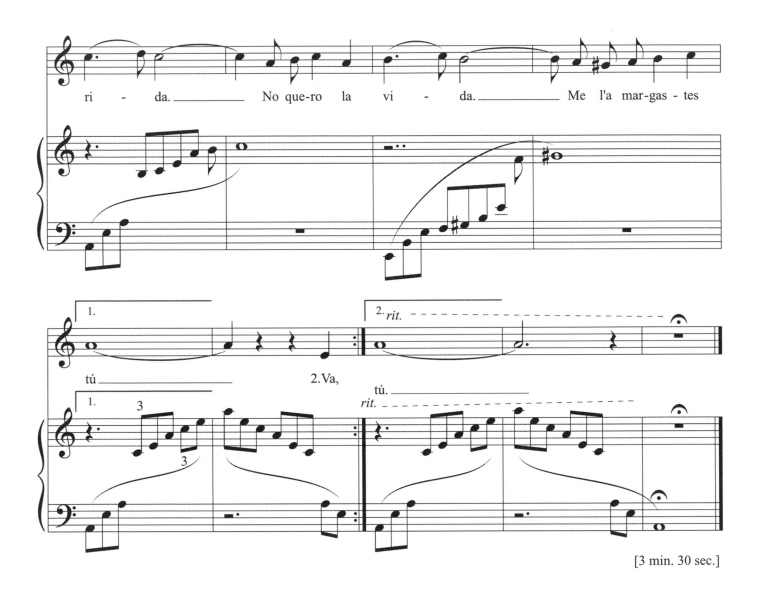

ri - da. _____ No que-ro la vi - da. _____ Me l'a mar-gas - tes

1. tú _____   2.Va,   tú. _____

[3 min. 30 sec.]

1. Your mother, when she bore you
   And brought you into this world,
   Did not give you a heart
   With which to love another.

   Goodbye, goodbye, beloved.
   I don't want to live.
   You have made me bitter.

2. Go, look for another love.
   Knock on other doors.
   Wait at other doors,
   Because, for me, you are dead.

   Goodbye, goodbye, beloved.
   I don't want to live.
   You have made me bitter.

26

Ah, el Novio No Quere Dinero

Arranged by
Samuel Milligan

Anonymous

Ah, el Novio No Quere Dinero

2.Ah, el no-vio_____ no que-re du-ca

dos. Ah, el no-vio_____ no que-re du-ca dos. Que-re a la no-via de ma-zal al-

to. Yo ven - go a ver que go-zen y lo-gren y ten-gan mu-cho_____

Ah, el Novio No Quere Dinero

bien.

3.Ah, el no - vio_____

no que-re ma-ni_____ llas.   Ah, el no-vio_____   no que-re ma-ni_____ llas. - Que re a la no -

via car' de a-le-gri-a.   Yo ven - go a ver que go - zen y lo -

29

Ah, el Novio No Quere Dinero

gren y ten-gen mu - cho____ bien.

a tempo

sfz

[1 min. 20 sec.]

1. Ah, the bridegroom doesn't want money. (2 times)
   He wants a bride of good fortune.
   I've come to look.
   May they be happy and have much good fortune.

2. Ah, the bridegroom doesn't want ducats. (2 times)
   He wants a bride of great fortune.
   I've come to look.
   May they be happy and have much good fortune.

3. Ah, the bridegroom doesn't want bracelets. (2 times)
   He wants a bride with a happy face.
   I've come to look.
   May they be happy and have much good fortune.

Arboles Lloran por Luvia

Arranged by
Samuel Milligan

Anonymous

Arboles Lloran por Luvia

o - jos por ti, que-ri-da a-man - te. An-si__ llo - ra el__ mi co-ra-

son, por ti, mi lin-da da - ma.

En fren - te de__

Arboles Lloran por Luvia

mi hay un án - ge - lo. Cuan - do

pa - sa, él me mi - ra. Ha - blar que - ro y no

pue - do, mi co - ra - son so - spi - ra. Ha - blar que - ro y no

Arboles Lloran por Luvia

pue - do, mi co - ra - son so - spi - ra.

[3 min. 5 sec.]

Trees cry for rain, and mountains for air.
So cry my eyes for you, dear love.
So cries my heart for you, my pretty lady.

In front of me is an angel.
When she passes she looks at me.
I want to speak, but cannot, my heart sighs.

La Rosa Enflorece

Arranged by
Samuel Milligan

Anonymous

Prepare G# II, III, and IV

La Rosa Enflorece

La Rosa Enflorece

La Rosa Enflorece

La Rosa Enflorece

pres - to ven ___ pa - lum - ba, más pres - to ven a ___ mi, más

pres - to tú ___ me ___ al - ma, que yo ___ me voy ___ mo -

rir, ___ mas pres - to tú mi al - ma, que

La Rosa Enflorece

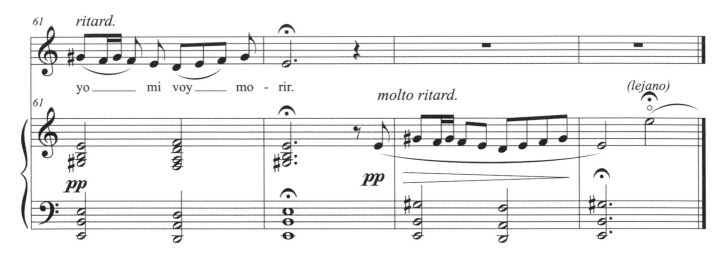

[3 min., 7 sec.]

The rose blossoms in the month of May,
And my soul is darkened, suffering for love;
And my soul is darkened, suffering for love.

The nightingales sing and sigh for love,
And passion kills me; great is my pain;
And passion kills me; great is my pain.

Come more quickly, dove, quickly come to me.
Quickly, my soul, for I am going to die;
Quickly, my soul, for I am going to die.

Note: *Notes with fingerings (22222) are played detached; that is, in ascending scale passages, muffle the first note of the series with the knuckle when playing the second note. Muffle the second when playing the third, etc.*

Como la Rosa en la Guerta

Arranged by
Samuel Milligan

Anonymous

41

Como la Rosa en la Guerta

co - mo la ro - sa en la güer - ta, y lasflo - res sin av -
tris - tes ho - ras en el di - a, que ha-zi - na ya ca -
su gra-ci - a y su mi - ra - da, e - ra mi con - so - la -

rir,___ an - si es u - na___ don - ce -
yó;___ co - mo la rey - na___ en su le -
ción.___ Al mi la - do se___ a - sen - ta -

la a las___ ho - ras___ del mu - rir.
cho, ya ca - yó y___ se dez ma - yo.
va, su ma - no___ en___ mi co - ra -

1, 2.

Como la Rosa en la Guerta

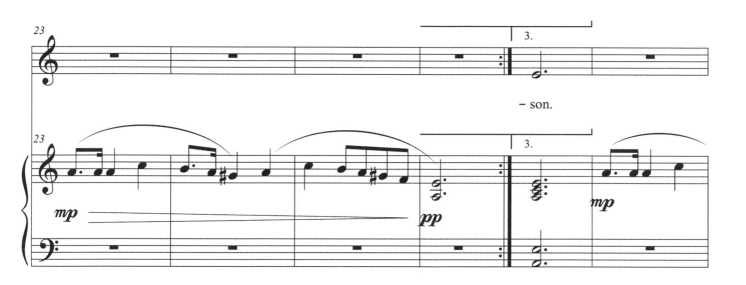

– son.

[3 min. 34 sec.]

1. Like a rose in the garden, and flowers not yet open,
   So is a maiden at the hour of death.

2. Sad hours in the day, when she fell into sickness.
   Like a queen on her couch, she fell and swooned away.

3. Your grace and your gaze were my consolation,
   When sitting at my side, your hand on my heart.

Note: *This is the intensely sad lament of a mother for a dead daughter. Curiously, it is generally sung by men, since it is thought to bring bad luck if sung by a woman. This stems from a desire, no doubt, to avoid tempting fate.*

(PERCUSSION)

Cuando el Rey Nimrod al Compo Salia

Arranged by
Samuel Milligan

Anonymous

44

Cuando el Rey Nimrod al Compo Salia

ta en la ju-de-ri - a. Que ha-vi-a de na-cer.___ Av - ra-ham a -
vi-nu. Av-ram a - vi - nu, pa-dre que-ri - do, padre ben-
di - cho,___ luz de Is-ra-el.___ Av-ram a vi-nu, pa-dre que-
ri - do, pa-dre ben - di - cho,___ luz de Is-ra - el. Sa-lu-

Cuando el Rey Nimrod al Compo Salia

Cuando el Rey Nimrod al Compo Salia

el._____ Av – ram a – vi – nu, pa – dre que – ri – do, pa – dre ben –

di – cho,__ luz de Is – ra – el. 3.Sa – lu – de – mos al com – pa – dre

y tam – bien al mo – el, que por su zek – hut mos__ ven – ga el go – el, y

ri' – ha – ma a to – do Is – ra – el. Ci – er – to__ lo – a – re – mos

Cuando el Rey Nimrod al Compo Salia

al___ ver - da - de - ro. Av - ram a - vi - nu, pa - dre que - ri - do, pa - dre ben -

di - cho,___ luz de Is - ra - el.___ Av - ram a - vi - nu, pa - dre que -

ri - do, pa - dre ben - di - cho, luz de Is - ra - el.

[1 min. 54 sec.]

About the Author/Arranger

The name of Samuel Milligan is one of the first that the beginning harp student is likely to encounter. When the harp making firm Lyon & Healy introduced their new Troubadour lever harp in 1961, they commissioned Milligan to furnish a new method, *Fun From the First,* plus another collection of pieces, *Medieval to Modern.* These have become standard repertory for harp students, and many pieces can be found as required material for harp contests and festivals. The introduction of the Troubadour harp and the publication of Milligan's music have been responsible, in large part, for the beginnings of the renaissance in harp playing that we see today. Where there was once little music for lever harp, there is now an abundance. Where there was only one maker of lever harps, there are now many.

Born in 1932 near Joplin, Missouri, he grew up in the Texas Panhandle. Even though sprung from such unlikely beginnings, Milligan's life was always defined by music. Both parents were enthusiastic singers, and he began piano lessons at age nine. However, his musical life began in earnest when he acquired a Clark Irish harp, which naturally fit the plans of his Irish father.

Harp scholarships allowed him to attend Del Mar Junior College in Corpus Christi, Texas, where he encountered his first real harp teacher, LaVerne Hodges Peterson, who installed a solid technique. He later transferred to North Texas State College (now the University of North Texas) where he received a Bachelor of Music degree with a major in harp performance. He began a master's degree in musicology, working with Dr. Helen Hewitt, who further fueled his fascination with early music, an interest first developed when he was in high school. However, the next year found him employed as a harp technician by Lyon & Healy in their New York City showroom. This enabled him to explore many avenues of harp playing, such as being a substitute on Broadway and at Radio City Music Hall, as well as much single-date playing, and a national tour with a chamber orchestra for Columbia Artists Management.

In the meantime, he began studies with Laura Newell, who had been Toscanini's first choice as harpist for his NBC Symphony. Milligan was impressed by her superb technique and musicianship. Among other things, she stressed economy of motion and careful finger placement to avoid any sibilants.

In 1967, at the request of Lucien Thomson, president of the American Harp Society, Milligan became the founding editor of the *American Harp Journal*, serving until 1971, afterwards contributing articles from time to time. He later served on the Boards of the American Harp Society and the Historical Harp Society, and was appointed by the AHS as a liaison between the two groups.

Since 2000, he has indulged his love for early Spanish music, an interest that had been encouraged years before by Nicanor Zabaleta, the Spanish harp virtuoso. For many years he organized various conjuntos for the performance of this music, the repertory covering the Medieval, Renaissance and Baroque periods, with emphasis on the music of the Spanish colonial New World. This involves much music for strictly diatonic harps, which Milligan defends by making a comparison to visual art, saying: "In the same way that a black and white drawing by Leonardo da Vinci is no less great art than any of his paintings in color, so a diatonic piece of music can be as artistically significant as something chromatic. In fact, economy of means can add to its artistic value."

Milligan has been the recipient of two recent awards. One, in 2008 from the American Harp Society, honors his outstanding service to the AHS and to the harp. Another, presented by the Somerset Harp Festival in 2014, is in honor of his lifetime achievement.

He currently lives in Brooklyn, New York, surrounded by harps of all sizes and descriptions.

Other titles by
Samuel Milligan

For lever or pedal harp

Fun From the First (a method in two volumes)

Medieval to Modern (repertory in three volumes)

Der Jolly Huntsman und der Kuckoo (for piccolo, harp and shotgun [slapstick])

Vox Cœlestis (five pieces for harp and organ)

For pedal harp

Vox Angelica (four pieces for harp and organ)

Black and White Rag by George Botsford

Kol Nidrei by Max Bruch (for cello, harp and organ)

Choral

Campanas de Belén / Bells of Bethlehem (for SATB choir and organ
with optional harp, handbells and glockenspiel)

Wings Press was founded in 1975 by Joanie Whitebird and Joseph F. Lomax, both deceased, as "an informal association of artists and cultural mythologists dedicated to the preservation of the literature of the nation of Texas." Publisher, editor and designer since 1995, Bryce Milligan is honored to carry on and expand that mission to include the finest in American writing—meaning all of the Americas, without commercial considerations clouding the decision to publish or not to publish.

Wings Press intends to produce multi-cultural books, chapbooks, ebooks, recordings and broadsides that enlighten the human spirit and enliven the mind. Everyone ever associated with Wings has been or is a writer, and we know well that writing is a transformational art form capable of changing the world, primarily by allowing us to glimpse something of each other's souls. We believe that good writing is innovative, insightful, and interesting. But most of all it is honest. As Bob Dylan put it, "To live outside the law, you must be honest."

Likewise, Wings Press is committed to treating the planet itself as a partner. Thus the press uses as much recycled material as possible, from the paper on which the books are printed to the boxes in which they are shipped.

As Robert Dana wrote in *Against the Grain*, "Small press publishing is personal publishing. In essence, it's a matter of personal vision, personal taste and courage, and personal friendships." Welcome to our world.

WINGS PRESS

Colophon

This first edition of *Nine Sephardic Songs*, by Samuel Milligan, has been printed on 60 pound Edwards Brothers paper containing a percentage of recycled fiber. Titles have been set in Pendragon FLF type, the text in Adobe Caslon type. This book was designed by Bryce Milligan.

On-line catalogue and ordering:
www.wingspress.com
Wings Press titles are distributed to the trade by the
Independent Publishers Group
www.ipgbook.com
and in Europe by Gazelle
www.gazellebookservices.co.uk

Also available as an ebook.